P9-BZC-666

# BEHOLD!
## *Spot-the-Difference Bible Stories*

Written by Wendy Madgwick
Illustrated by Hemesh Alles

Random House New York

First American edition, 1994.

Copyright © 1994 by The Templar Company plc.

All rights reserved under International and Pan-American Copyright
Conventions. Published in the United States by Random House, Inc., New York.
Devised and produced by The Templar Company plc,
Pippbrook Mill, London Road, Dorking, Surrey RH4 1JE, Great Britain.
Designed by Janie Louise Hunt

**Library of Congress Cataloging in Publication Data**
Madgwick, Wendy.
Behold! : spot-the-difference bible stories / by Wendy Madgwick;
illustrated by Hemesh Alles.—1st American ed.
p. cm.
Summary: Scenes from the Old Testament are depicted in pairs of plates,
the second plate in each pair containing ten differences to be spotted by the
reader. Includes a simple account of each story.
ISBN 0-679-85333-2
1. Bible stories, English—O.T. [Bible stories—O.T. 2. Picture puzzles.]
I. Alles, Hemesh, ill. II. Title.
BS551.2.M298 1993
221.9'505—dc20
93-5506

Manufactured in Italy
1 2 3 4 5 6 7 8 9 10

# INTRODUCTION

Each pair of paintings in this colorful collection
of Bible stories may seem the same, but look again and
Behold! ten changes will be revealed. The dove
has returned to the ark with an olive branch in its beak;
the flames on the altar are higher.
Can you spot each difference? If you need help,
turn the page and all will become clear — you'll find the
answer key and a simple telling of the Bible story.
Get ready to test your powers of observation — and
discover some of the greatest stories ever told!

# FORTY DAYS OF RAIN

# Noah's Ark

1. There are two parrots.
2. The dove is carrying an olive branch.
3. The sun is shining through the clouds.
4. Mountain tops can be seen.
5. Noah's beard is longer.
6. Dolphins are playing.
7. The sea is calmer.
8. One elephant is feeding.
9. The tunic has changed color.
10. A polar bear is missing.

*The story of Noah and the great flood is one of the best-known tales from the Bible. The exciting events that unfold in Genesis, Chapter 6, have been retold worldwide in stories, songs, and poems.*

Long ago, in the time of Noah, the world was an evil place. The people had forgotten God and no longer praised him or followed his ways.

All, that is, except for one man — Noah. Noah was a good, kind man who, forever thankful to God for his loving wife and three sons, prayed to God daily.

God, looking down upon this beautiful world which he had created, was angry.

"I will destroy the world," thought God. Then, seeing Noah, he repented. "No, I will save that which is good — Noah's family and the innocent animals that inhabit the earth."

So God spoke to Noah, warning him that a flood was coming to wash away all evil. He told Noah to build a huge wooden ark

three hundred cubits long. "Save yourself and your family," said the Lord, "and gather a male and female of each wild creature so that they too may be saved."

So Noah and his family built the ark and filled it with food as God had told them. Noah's neighbors laughed at him, calling him names, but Noah did not care. He and his sons collected animals of every kind from throughout the Earth. And two by two a multitude of creatures walked, crawled, slithered, wriggled, and flew into the ark. From the ferocious lions of the jungle to the gentle lambs of the field, all were gathered in. When they were all settled, Noah and his family drew up the gangplank and battened down the hatch.

Then the rain started. Huge drops smashed into the ground and sprayed dust into the air. For forty days and forty nights it rained. The land became awash with waves — one enormous sea on which the ark sailed safely. Everything else on Earth perished.

After many weeks, God remembered Noah and sent a great wind to dry up the flood. As the wind blew and the sun shone, the seas slowly dried up. Eventually the ark came to rest on the top of Mount Ararat. But Noah did not know if it was safe to leave the ark. Noah opened a window and let loose a raven, but the bird did not return. A few days later, he sent forth a dove — but it too returned. A week later Noah tried again. The dove once again winged its way home, but this time it carried a sign of life — a fresh, green olive branch.

Then God told Noah it was time to leave the ark.

"At last," sighed Noah as he freed the animals. Gathering his family around him, Noah thanked God for delivering them from harm. God spoke once more to Noah.

"Look to the sky, Noah, for a sign of my promise to you. Never again shall I send a flood to destroy the Earth and its people. Whenever the sun breaks through rain clouds my sign will shine forth to remind everyone of my pledge."

Noah turned. Before him, clear for all to see, was God's sign: a glowing multicolored archway that linked Heaven and Earth — a rainbow.

1. Joseph has his staff of office.
2. The spear is now a fan.
3. There is a chain between Simeon's ankles.
4. A bag of grain is now gold.
5. There is a second guard.
6. There is another donkey.
7. One of Joseph's brothers is wearing different clothes.
8. The lion's mane is different.
9. The carving on the temple wall has changed.
10. A camel train has arrived.

*The story of Joseph and how God helped him rise to power in Egypt after his brothers' betrayal has been the subject of many plays — and even a musical! You can read the full story in the Book of Genesis, Chapters 37–46.*

There was famine in many lands, and people were starving. Only Egypt had food, and soon people in nearby countries heard of it. The news reached Canaan, where a man named Jacob lived. He called his eleven sons to him and told them to go to Egypt to buy grain. Ten of his sons set out; the youngest, Benjamin, stayed at home.

When at last the brothers arrived, they were taken to Pharaoh's overseer, Joseph, whose job was to sell the grain. Joseph stared at the men. He knew them right away — they were his brothers! As he looked at them, his past flashed before him. He remembered how his jealous brothers had sold him into slavery. But God had given Joseph the gift of explaining dreams. He had come to Pharaoh's

attention when he told of the famine and described how the food should be stored. Now Joseph was Pharaoh's trusted adviser. The brothers did not recognize Joseph. Why should they? They thought he was dead. And anyway he was dressed as an Egyptian and pretended not to understand their language. "Where are you from?" Joseph asked through a translator.

"We come from Canaan," they replied. But Joseph accused them of being spies.

"No!" they cried. "We come from a family of twelve brothers. One is dead and the youngest, Benjamin, is at home."

Joseph demanded that they bring Benjamin to him to prove that they were telling the truth. Then he ordered that one brother, Simeon, be held prisoner until the others returned. Not realizing he could understand them, the brothers cried out in despair that this was their punishment for betraying Joseph. Then, loading up their donkeys with grain, they set out for Canaan.

When the brothers got home they found a money bag in each sack of corn, put there by Joseph to test them. "Now they will call us thieves as well as spies!" they cried in despair. "We dare not go back!" But soon the grain ran out. Reluctantly they returned to Egypt to buy more food, taking Benjamin with them.

They stood fearfully before Joseph and explained about the money. To their surprise, Joseph was kind. He released Simeon and ordered that their sacks be refilled. The brothers set off for home again but they had not gone far when Joseph's servant overtook them, crying, "Thieves! You have stolen my master's best cup." Sure enough, Joseph had put the precious goblet in Benjamin's bag. There it lay, gleaming among the grain.

Silently, the brothers returned to the city, terrified of what Joseph would do. They were dismayed when he ordered Benjamin to become his slave. "No, my lord," pleaded Judah, the fourth brother. "Take me instead. It would kill my father if he lost Benjamin." His brothers' anguish pierced Joseph's heart and he told them then that he was their brother. At first they were terrified but Joseph said, "What happened in the past was God's wish." And they knew then that they had been forgiven.

# THE GOLDEN CALF

1. A stone tablet is missing.
2. The mountaintop is misty.
3. A dancer is wearing a gold necklace.
4. The golden calf is covered with a cloth.
5. The flames are higher.
6. A man is holding a sword.
7. A sheep is by the altar.
8. A man is praying.
9. There is an extra tree.
10. A tent is missing.

*Thousands of years ago, God made an agreement with Moses that he would care for the people of Israel if they kept his laws. Those laws were the Ten Commandments, which many people still live by today. You can read about them in the Book of Exodus, Chapters 19–34.*

The Israelites were on their way to the Promised Land. They had traveled from Egypt to Mount Sinai. They set up camp and Moses, their leader, climbed Mount Sinai to pray. There God spoke to him. "Tell the Israelites that I will care for them if they obey my laws," God said. "In three days I will speak to you in front of them. Go now, and prepare them for my coming."

Moses hurried back to the camp to give God's message to the people. On the morning of the third day, they gathered to listen to God. Fiery smoke billowed from the mountaintop, and thunder crashed all around. The Israelites became frightened. Then there was a loud trumpet call, and God spoke to Moses in a voice like thunder. The terrified

Israelites backed away, leaving Moses alone. The Lord said:

"These are my Ten Commandments, which you must live by."

- *You must not worship any other God but me.*
- *You must not worship false idols.*
- *You must not take my name in vain.*
- *Remember to keep the Sabbath day holy.*
- *Honor your father and mother.*
- *You shall not kill.*
- *You shall not commit adultery.*
- *You shall not steal.*
- *You shall not bear false witness against others.*
- *You shall not desire other people's property.*

Then God departed, and Moses told the Israelites that they would be God's special people if they promised to obey his laws. The people agreed. Then God summoned Moses once again to the mountain, to receive two stone tablets that had God's Commandments written on them.

Weeks passed, and Moses did not return.

The Israelites grew restless and, certain that they would never see Moses again, they turned to his brother, Aaron. "Make a god for us to worship!" they demanded. So Aaron took all their gold jewelry and melted it down. From the gold he made an idol — a golden calf. "Here is our god!" the people shouted. The next day, they offered sacrifices to the calf and danced around it. God saw that they had broken their promise and was angry. "Arise Moses," he said. "Your people have broken my laws."

Moses hurried back to the camp, carrying the two stone tablets. When he saw the Israelites dancing around the golden calf, he was furious. He threw the tablets down, and they smashed to pieces. Moses seized the golden calf and turned to Aaron. "Why did you let them do this?" he said.

"It's not my fault," Aaron pleaded. "They demanded a god."

The next day, Moses gathered together all the Israelites who wanted to follow God. Then he climbed Mount Sinai again to beg God's forgiveness. This time the people waited patiently. They were happy when Moses returned with two more stone tablets — and God's forgiveness. They celebrated and built a temple to God, as he had commanded. Then they went on their way to the Promised Land.

# THE WALLS FALL DOWN

1. The ram's horn is in a different position.
2. There is a crack in the wall.
3. The sun is setting.
4. The gold poles are now wooden.
5. Another Israelite is shouting.
6. There is an extra palm tree.
7. There is a lamb near the wall.
8. The tower has an extra window.
9. The priest's headdress has a striped band.
10. A spear is missing.

*The story of Joshua and the Battle of Jericho is told in the Book of Joshua, Chapters 5–6 and shows God's power in all its glory.*

Moses died before the Israelites reached the Promised Land, and God chose Joshua to lead them the rest of the way. The Israelites had safely crossed over the river Jordan, and now they were camped outside the beautiful city of Jericho.

The king of Jericho had watched as the tribes of Israel set up camp outside his city walls. He locked and barred the city gates and warned his guards not to let any strangers enter. He instructed the leaders of his army to get ready for an attack. Then he waited to see what the Israelites would do.

God had told Joshua that the Israelites had to capture Jericho before they could enter the Promised Land. One day, as Joshua stood looking

at the city, he noticed a man who was carrying a sword. The man was watching him. Joshua called out, "Who are you, and what do you want? Are you one of my soldiers or are you an enemy?"

"The Lord God sent me," the man answered. "Take off your sandals; this place is holy." Then Joshua knew that the stranger was a messenger from God. The man told Joshua to trust in God and do exactly what God wanted. He went on to explain in detail what Joshua must do. Joshua was amazed at the battle plan but promised to follow God's orders. He knew that he could trust in him.

Joshua returned to the camp and sent for seven priests. "God has commanded that once a day for six days you must walk around the city walls," he told them. "You must march in front of the Ark of the Covenant, the great gold chest that contains the tablets inscribed with God's

law, and you must carry seven ram's horns as trumpets." Then Joshua sent for the army and the rest of the Israelites. He ordered armed soldiers to walk in front of the priests and more soldiers

to march behind.

So the priests, soldiers, and Israelites did as they were told and marched once around the city of Jericho, then returned to their camp. The second day they did the same. The people of Jericho were bewildered. "When are they going to attack?" they asked themselves, but no attack came.

For six days the Israelites marched once around Jericho and then returned quietly to their camp. Then on the seventh day, Joshua called the Israelites to him.

"Today," he said, "you must march seven times around the city walls. Then the priests will blow their horns and you must all shout out. Shout at the top of your lungs, because God has given you the city."

One...twice...three times the Israelites marched, and the people of Jericho watched from the city walls. Four...five...six times. The seventh time, the priests blew their horns and the people shouted with all their might. At first the walls seemed to shimmer in the heat. Then they trembled and shook and came tumbling down! With cries of victory, Joshua and the Israelites entered the city.

# Samson in the Temple

1. Samson has longer hair.
2. Samson's eyes are open and he is calling out to God.
3. Samson's leg chain is broken.
4. The pillar has a bigger crack.
5. The roof arch has a golden ball.
6. The boy is holding a rope.
7. The goblet is now silver.
8. The god Dagon's statue is different.
9. The flames are higher.
10. A Philistine is running away.

*The story of Samson and his amazing strength can be found in the Book of Judges, Chapters 13–16. His downfall at the hands of Delilah and the eventual destruction of his enemies have been retold in folk tales throughout the world.*

Long ago, in the land of Canaan, lived an Israelite named Manoah. Life was very hard for the Israelites, because they were ruled by the powerful Philistines. The Israelites prayed for God to send a leader to help them. Manoah and his wife longed for something else as well — a son.

One day, a messenger from God appeared to Manoah's wife. "You have prayed for a son for years," he said, "and soon your wish will be granted. He will be very special, and his great strength will help deliver Israel from the Philistines. But from the day he is born, he is to be dedicated to God. And, remember, you must *never* cut his hair."

When their son was born, Manoah and his wife called him Samson. He grew up to be amazingly

strong and could defeat anyone in combat. He even killed a young lion with his bare hands when it attacked him. Samson was treated very badly by the Philistines and for many years he fought against them, killing many of their soldiers.

After some time, Samson became a judge and helped to govern Israel, but the Philistines continued to plan his downfall. Their chance came when Samson fell in love with a beautiful woman called Delilah. The Philistine chieftains promised Delilah great wealth if she could discover the secret of Samson's strength. She begged Samson to tell her, but again and again he refused. At last, worn down by her continual questions, he revealed that his strength lay in his long hair, which symbolized his vow to dedicate his life to God.

That night Delilah lulled Samson to sleep, his head on her lap. She called to a Philistine soldier who was standing nearby.

Silently the man cut off Samson's hair and beard. Gazing down on his shorn head, Delilah cried, "The Philistines are upon you, Samson!"

Samson arose laughing and braced himself for the onslaught. But his strength had vanished, and the Philistine soldiers overcame him. They bound him and took him to Gaza where, after blinding him, they imprisoned him in chains.

One day, in thanks to their god Dagon, the Philistines arranged a huge feast in their temple. They shouted for Samson to entertain them. A slave boy guided the blind champion through the jeering throng to the central pillars. Samson took no notice of his enemies and their victory song. His shorn hair had begun to grow again, and his mighty strength was returning. And now his mind was filled with one thought — the Philistines' destruction. Placing his hands on the two main supporting pillars, Samson prayed to God to give him back his strength. Then he bowed his head and pushed with all his might. At first the pillars merely trembled. But then they began to crumble. The terrified Philistines tried to flee, but it was too late. The magnificent temple collapsed, killing everyone within. Samson did not escape. The Israelite hero died with his enemies, a prayer to God on his lips.

# David and Goliath

1. David's bag has a flap and tassels.
2. David's sling has changed position.
3. Goliath's leg armor is higher.
4. Goliath's spear is different.
5. Goliath's sword hilt is a different color.
6. Goliath's shield has a different pattern.
7. A Philistine's spear is missing.
8. An eagle is flying in the sky.
9. An Israelite's shield is missing.
10. A Philistine's banner has changed color.

*The famous story of David the giant killer is widely recognized in songs and poems as a symbol of right overcoming might. You can read about David's battle with Goliath in I Samuel, Chapter 17.*

The Israelites had been at war with the Philistines for many years. The two armies had gathered for battle and were camped on opposite sides of a valley.

One day, David's father told him to take food to his three brothers who were in the Israelite army. David was happy to go because he had never been to the battlefront. He was only a shepherd boy.

David arrived at the edge of the camp just as the soldiers were going into battle. He was about to go in search of his brothers when a hush fell upon the soldiers, and all eyes turned toward the Philistines.

David looked across the valley. He could hardly believe what he saw. Before him stood the largest man he had ever seen — a giant,

fully armed for battle. The giant strode to the edge of the valley and roared to the waiting Israelites:

"Come, you cowards. Pick a champion. If he wins, we will serve you. But if *I* kill *him*, you will be our slaves!"

"Who is this man?" demanded David.

"That is Goliath," a soldier replied. "He challenges us every day but none dare to fight him."

Sure enough, David saw that the Israelite soldiers were running back into their camp and he was angry.

"How can you stand by and let this man insult the army of the Lord?" he raged, and the soldiers who heard him were impressed by his anger and fearlessness.

Saul, the king of the Israelites, heard of David's speech and sent for him.

"I will fight this Goliath," said David.

"You!" said the king in astonishment. "Don't be foolish. You're only a boy." But David was determined.

"As a shepherd, I have killed both lions and bears when they stole a lamb from my flock," replied David.

"Then go, and the Lord be with you," said Saul. He clothed David in his own armor and gave him his mighty sword. But David could hardly move.

"I cannot wear these," David said, and handed them back.

Instead, he went to a nearby brook, still carrying his shepherd's staff. He chose five smooth stones and put them in his bag. Then, with his slingshot in his hand, he bravely walked out to meet the giant Goliath.

"Am I a dog that you come with a stick to beat me!" Goliath cried angrily. "Come! I will give your dead body to the birds of the air and the beasts of the field."

"You come to me with your great sword and spear," replied David, "but I come to you in the name of the Lord God and he will give me victory over you. It is Philistine flesh that will feed the birds and beasts today."

With that, David ran forward. He placed a stone in his slingshot and flung it at the giant with deadly accuracy. It struck him in the forehead and he fell on his face, senseless. David ran over, drew Goliath's great sword, and killed him. When the Philistines saw that the mighty Goliath was dead, they fled from the land of Israel.

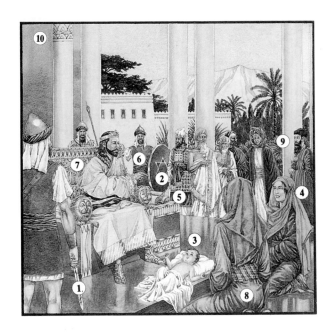

1. The servant has a sword.
2. Solomon is pointing his finger.
3. The baby has woken up.
4. The mother is smiling.
5. There is another scroll.
6. Solomon's staff of office is different.
7. The throne has jewels on it.
8. The woman's sash has a different pattern.
9. The man's beard is black.
10. The pillar has a pattern at the top.

*In ancient times, the name of Solomon was a watchword for wisdom, and so it is today. You can find out about the golden age of Solomon and the wise decisions he made in I Kings, Chapters 3–12 of the Old Testament.*

**K**ing David was growing old, and so he proclaimed his son Solomon as his successor. When David died, Solomon became king of Israel.

One day, Solomon went on a pilgrimage, or holy journey, to Gibeon to pray and praise God. That night he had a dream. God appeared to him and asked him what gift he would most like. Solomon knew at once and asked to be blessed with wisdom. "For I am young," he said, "and cannot rule Israel unless you help me."

God was pleased with Solomon's request and said, "I shall certainly give you a wise and understanding heart — you will be the wisest man that ever lived. Also, because you did not ask, I will give you great riches and glory. And, if you

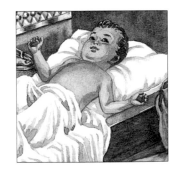

keep my laws, you will have a long life."

Solomon awoke and knew that, although he had only been dreaming, God would help him to be a wise and just king.

God fulfilled the promise and Solomon became famous far and wide for his wisdom and knowledge, and his skills and patience at court. Many of his subjects sought his help.

One day, two women came to seek his advice. They were shown into the throne room, where Solomon held court. As they entered, one woman tried to snatch a bundle from the arms of another. But the other woman held the bundle tightly. Suddenly it began to wriggle and cry, and Solomon saw that it was a baby. A courtier gently took the child, soothing it until it fell asleep. The women stood before the king to tell their story.

"We live in the same house," began one of the women. "I gave birth to a son and,

three days later, this woman also had a child. One night she lay on her child by accident and smothered him. Then, while I was sleeping, she crept into my room and took my living son from my arms and put her dead child in his place. When I woke up, I found the dead child. But then I realised it was not mine but hers!"

"No! No!" cried the other woman. "The dead baby was yours. This is *my* son!"

Solomon let them argue for a few minutes, then he held up his hand for silence.

"So, you both claim this child is yours," he said, and turned to his courtier. "Put the babe here in front of me," he instructed, "and go fetch a sword. Since both these women claim the babe, cut the boy in two and give them each half."

At once, the baby's true mother cried out, "No! No! Give her the living child. Don't put him to death!"

But the other woman was already saying, "Neither mine nor yours shall he be. Cut the babe in two!"

"Stop!" ordered Solomon. "Give the child to the woman who wants to spare his life. She is the true mother."
At that the real mother, smiling with joy, bent and picked up her son.

Soon all of Jerusalem had heard about the case, and all gave thanks for their wise and clever king.

1. There is another piece of meat on Baal's altar.
2. A guard is holding a priest.
3. The pile of wood is smaller.
4. The water has dried up.
5. A barrel of water is missing.
6. An altar stone is crumbling
7. A man is kneeling to pray.
8. The pattern on Elijah's sash is different.
9. The flames on the altar are higher.
10. The sky is dark with rain.

*The story of Elijah shows how faith can help one overcome obstacles. You can read how God guided Elijah and sent fire from heaven to show his power in I Kings, Chapter 18.*

In Elijah's time, the land of Israel was ruled by King Ahab and his wife, Jezebel. Jezebel had been a princess in a country where they worshipped a god called Baal. When she came to Israel, she wanted Baal to be the only god and she had many of the Lord God's prophets killed. King Ahab built a temple to Baal and many Israelites turned away from the Lord to worship this new god.

During Ahab's reign there lived a prophet named Elijah. He lived in hiding from Ahab and Jezebel because he had sent them a warning that drought would cripple Israel for many years, and it had.

Three years passed until one day God told Elijah to show himself to the king and rain would

once again return to the land. So Elijah met with Ahab and presented him with a challenge.

"Bring the Israelites to Mount Carmel," Elijah told him. "Then we shall see who is the true god — the God of Israel or Baal."

The next morning, King Ahab called together the Israelites and the prophets of Baal, and together they went to Mount Carmel. Elijah was waiting for them. He stepped forward and spoke.

"When will you decide which god you will worship?" he asked the Israelites. "It is time you made up your minds. I am the only prophet of the Lord here, but there are four hundred and fifty prophets of Baal. I issue them this challenge: build an altar to your god and put wood on it. Prepare a bull as a sacrifice and put it on top of the wood. Then call upon Baal to set fire to your offering."

The prophets of Baal prepared their

altar and sacrifice just as Elijah had said. Then they began to pray but nothing happened. They danced around the altar and shouted out loud. They begged Baal to hear their pleas. But the

day passed and still nothing happened.

"Now it is my turn," Elijah said. First he built an altar of stone to God and placed a pile of wood upon it. Then he dug a trench around the altar and called for water. Elijah poured four precious barrels of water over the altar, the wood, and the sacrifice. More water was brought until it ran off the altar and filled the trench. Then Elijah raised his arms to heaven.

"Lord God," Elijah said, "hear your humble servant. Send fire to show that you are the one true God."

Flames lit the altar immediately and burned the sacrifice and the wood. The fire burned so hard that it destroyed the stones of the altar. It dried up the water in the trench, and scorched the earth around the altar. The people who witnessed this miracle fell to their knees, praising God and begging his forgiveness. Then Elijah told the Israelites to seize the prophets of Baal. They would be put to death to free Israel from their evil influence.

Elijah looked up at the sky. There were rain clouds gathering in the west. The Lord God had kept his promise.

# THE WRITING ON THE WALL

1. The spear is missing.
2. Daniel is clothed in scarlet.
3. The writing on the wall is complete.
4. Daniel is pointing at the writing.
5. The gold goblet is now silver.
6. A candle is burning.
7. The wine is spilled.
8. The pattern on the tablecloth has changed.
9. The woman's headdress is different.
10. There is an extra plate of food.

*The story of the mysterious hand that wrote
on the wall and then disappeared is very famous.
You can read about the words and their meaning in the
Book of Daniel, Chapter 5.*

Belshazzar, the king of Babylon, decided one day to give a feast for his noblemen and their wives. It was a lavish banquet, and everyone ate and drank a great deal. As Belshazzar was drinking a goblet of wine, he had an idea. "Bring me the gold and silver cups and bowls that my father, Nebuchadnezzar, took from the holy temple at Jerusalem," he ordered.

"We will drink to our gods and goddesses."

The servants brought him the cups, and the noblemen and women drank from them. They praised the gods of gold and silver, bronze and iron, wood and stone.

Suddenly, King Belshazzar stopped. He turned and stared at the wall behind him. A mysterious hand had appeared and was

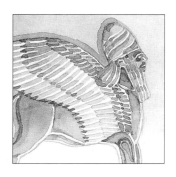

writing on the wall! Belshazzar shook with fear and pointed. The noblemen and women were silent as they watched the hand move slowly across the wall.

"Bring the wise men!" the king shouted. "Anyone who can explain this will get a big reward."

But the wise men had no idea what the words meant. The king became frightened and called for someone to help him. The queen, his mother, tried to calm him.

"There is a well-known prophet named Daniel," she said. "He explained many dreams for your father, Nebuchadnezzar. Perhaps he can interpret the writing. Send for him."

So Daniel was brought before the king and was offered great wealth if he could explain the strange writing.

"I do not want your gifts," Daniel replied. "I will tell you what these words mean because they come from God. You ignored God when you could have learned of his greatness from your father. You saw how Nebuchadnezzar's pride led to his downfall. But you learned nothing. You have even used the

holy goblets from God's temple at your drunken feast. You have toasted your false gods with them, and so the Lord has sent you a message. Perhaps this time you will listen to him.

"Let me tell you what he says. The words 'Mene, Mene, Tekel, U-Pharsin' mean 'numbered, numbered, weighted and divided.' *'Mene'* means God has numbered the days of your kingdom, and they are coming to an end. *'Tekel'* means you have been weighed on God's scales and have been found wanting. And the final word, *'U-Pharsin'*, tells you that your kingdom will be divided up and given to your enemies — the Medes and Persians."

Belshazzar was dismayed, but he knew that Daniel was speaking the truth. He kept his promise and rewarded Daniel by clothing him in scarlet and putting a gold chain around his neck. Belshazzar then made Daniel the third ruler in the kingdom.

That very night enemy troops stormed the city walls. They overran Babylon and killed Belshazzar. Darius the Mede became the new king. Everything Daniel had said came true.

# A STORM AT SEA

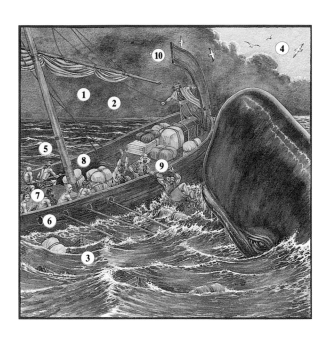

1. There is a rolled-up sail.
2. The lightning has disappeared.
3. Another crate has been thrown overboard.
4. The sun is appearing from behind the clouds.
5. The sea is calmer.
6. An oar is missing.
7. A sailor is praying.
8. A bundle is missing from the deck.
9. Jonah's cap is missing.
10. The bow is a different shape.

*The story of Jonah is well known the world over —
how he disobeyed God and was saved from drowning by
being swallowed by a huge fish. You can read more in the
Book of Jonah, Chapters 1–3.*

One day, long ago, God spoke to his prophet Jonah.

"Go to the great city of Nineveh," God told Jonah. "Warn them to repent and stop their wicked ways. Otherwise I will punish them."

But Jonah did not want to go and preach in Nineveh, because the people there were fierce and war-like.

"If I go to Nineveh and give them God's message," Jonah thought, "they may do as he has commanded and repent, begging his forgiveness. Because the Lord is a kind and merciful God, he will forgive them, and they will not be punished. That cannot be right, for they are wicked and deserve God's anger."

So Jonah decided to disobey God. He traveled to the seaport of Joppa, where he found a

ship bound for Tarshish, far away from Nineveh. "God will not find me there," thought Jonah to himself. So he paid his fare and climbed on board. He went to his cabin and, weary after his journey, fell asleep.

The ship set sail, but no sooner had it left the safety of the port when a mighty storm arose. Waves rose higher and higher, crashing against the ship's bow and washing over the deck. The captain went below to check on his passenger and found Jonah sleeping, unaware of the raging storm.

"Wake up!" the captain cried. "Pray to God for help, or surely we shall all die!"

The sailors feared that the ship would break up. They threw the cargo overboard to lighten the load and make the ship easier to control, but the storm grew worse. The sailors believed that Jonah was to blame for their trouble and when they accused him, Jonah confessed.

"I worship the God who made Heaven and Earth. I am his prophet, but I have disobeyed him," he said.

"How can we put things right?" the frightened sailors asked.

"By casting me into the sea," Jonah replied.

But the sailors were kind men and did not want to harm Jonah. They bent their backs to the oars and rowed hard to bring the ship to shore, but they could not. They cried aloud to Jonah's God, begging him for forgiveness but still the storm raged. So the sailors picked Jonah up and threw him into the raging sea. At once the wind died down and the seas grew calmer. As the sailors watched, a dark shape loomed up from beneath the foaming waters. It was a huge fish, and it opened its great mouth wide and swallowed Jonah whole. The sailors prayed to God and promised him that they would do his will. Then they rowed for shore to tell everyone what they had seen.

For three days and nights, Jonah stayed in the great whale's belly. He prayed to God constantly, asking forgiveness and promising to do God's will. On the third day, the fish swam close to land, and God commanded it to deliver Jonah up safely on the shore.

"Go to Nineveh, Jonah," God commanded.

"According to your will, Lord," replied Jonah humbly, and he went to Nineveh. He had learned his lesson and would never again defy God.